D0298141

Oh Boris!

Published in 2016 by Dog 'n' Bone Books
An imprint of Ryland Peters & Small Ltd

20–21 Jockey's Fields   341 E 116th St
London WC1R 4BW   New York, NY 10029
www.rylandpeters.com

10 9 8 7 6 5 4 3 2 1

Text, design, and illustration © Dog 'n' Bone Books 2016
Picture credits: page 45 Getty Images

All rights reserved. No part of this publication may be
reproduced, stored in a retrieval system, or transmitted
in any form or by any means, electronic, mechanical,
photocopying, or otherwise, without the prior permission of
the publisher.

A CIP catalog record for this book is available from
the Library of Congress and the British Library.

ISBN: 978 1 911026 18 1

Printed in China

Designer: Geoff Borin
Illustrator: Blair Frame

Compiled and written by: Pete Jorgensen and Penny Craig
Art director: Sally Powell
Head of production: Patricia Harrington
Publisher: Cindy Richards

Contents

A Brief History of Boris

Here's a very brief timeline of the highs and lows of BoJo's career.

◆✦ Despite being perceived as quintessentially British, Boris was in fact born in New York City on June 19th 1964 to Stanley, a politician, writer and environmentalist, and Charlotte, a painter.

◆✦ As a child, Boris's family moved around a lot and by the age of 10 he had lived at several London addresses, and in Oxford, Washington D.C., Connecticut and Brussels. Worryingly, as a small boy Boris Johnson's dream job was to be World King.

◆✦ Boris won a scholarship to Eton, one of the most prestigious schools on the planet. He made the most of his time at the school, becoming editor of the school newspaper, secretary of the debating society and earning himself a place at Oxford University.

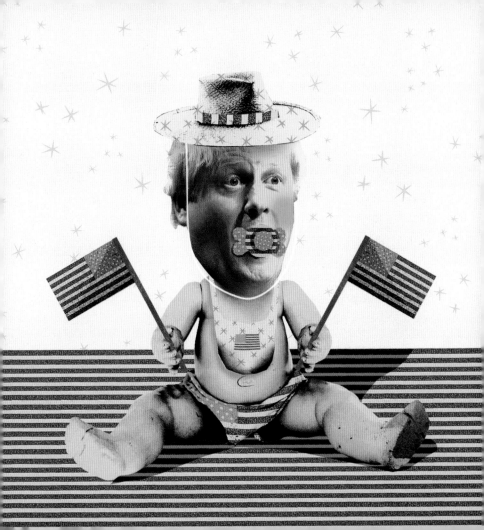

◆✦ After a gap year spent in Australia, Boris studied Classics at Balliol College. It was here that he began his associations with future Conservative Prime Minister David Cameron, and both were members of the infamous Bullingdon Club, a hard-drinking group for upper class students known for smashing up restaurants. BoJo later described it as "a truly shameful vignette of almost superhuman undergraduate arrogance, toffishness and twittishness."

◆✦ At Oxford, Boris became President of the Oxford Union. It was also during this time that he began to cultivate his bumbling buffoon persona.

◆✦ Upon graduating in 1987, Boris married his first wife Allegra Mostyn-Owen, who he met during his first term at Oxford. The story goes he turned up to her room for a party, but on the wrong night. On their wedding day Boris brought the wrong outfit so had to get married in borrowed clothes. He also managed to lose his wedding ring later that evening.

◆✦ Boris's first job was working for a management consultancy firm— he jacked it in after a week and secured a position at *The Times*. Boris was sacked from his job as a journalist at the paper for making up a quote.

◆✦ Boris's next appointment was for *The Daily Telegraph* and in 1989 he moved to Brussels to cover the European Commission. His Eurosceptic columns were a hit with many right-leaning readers and caused chaos between pro- and anti-EU factions of the Tory party. In his own words: "Everything I wrote from Brussels was having this amazing, explosive effect on the Tory party, and it really gave me this I suppose rather weird sense of power."

◆✦ His popularity saw him promoted to chief political columnist for *The Telegraph* and become a regular on TV show *Have I Got News for You*, further raising his public profile. In 1999 he was appointed as editor of *The Spectator*.

◆✦ Although he had cultivated a very successful career in the media, Boris still harbored strong political ambitions. During the 1997 general election he failed in his attempt to become MP for the Labour safe seat of Clwyd South. However, success came four years later when he was declared MP for Henley at the 2001 general election.

◆✦ Boris's early years as an MP weren't the smoothest. He was appointed Shadow Arts Minister but was later sacked following accusations of an affair, which Johnson initially denied but which was later proved to be true. This didn't stop him from increasing his majority in Henley during the 2005 general election, and he was given a new position as Shadow Higher Education Secretary.

◆✦ In 2008 Boris successfully ran against Ken Livingstone in the election to become London Mayor, winning 53.2% of the vote. He was elected for a second term in 2012.

◆✦ During his time as Mayor, Johnson oversaw several major initiatives, including the introduction of "Boris bikes," the replacement of "bendy buses" with new Routemasters, and the hosting of the 2012 London Olympics, all while continuously increasing his public profile (for better or worse, depending on who you talk to).

◆✦ 2016 saw Boris step down from his mayoral position, having been elected as MP for Uxbridge and South Ruislip the previous year. Also in 2016, Boris became one of the chief architects of Brexit, successfully campaigning for Britain to leave the EU.

◆✦ Following the referendum, Boris went from favorite to be the new Prime Minister to having his chances scuppered when he was politically outmaneuvered by Michael Gove. Just as the political wilderness beckoned, new PM Theresa May appointed him Foreign Secretary, much to the disbelief of statespeople both at home and abroad. During his two-year stint as Foreign Secretary, Boris likened the French President to a World War II prison guard, called Africa a country rather than a continent, and managed to insult the whole of Italy.

◆✦ In 2018, Boris quit as Foreign Secretary, stating that to support Mrs May's government was not in his the country's best interest. He resurfaced in 2019 to launch a successful bid to become PM. At the time of writing (30 minutes after his victory was announced), he hasn't yet managed to cock things up.

Post-truth Facts

During the campaign for Brexit, Boris and his cohorts ushered in a new era of post-truth politics. Can you separate the Boris-related facts below from the fiction?

1. Boris' paternal grandfather was a Turkish journalist and newspaper editor who was rather gruesomely beaten to death during the Turkish War of Independence.

☐ TRUE ☐ FALSE

2. He is a direct descendent of George II—his great-great-great-great-great-great-great-great-grandfather, and is a distant relative of the Queen.

☐ TRUE ☐ FALSE

3. Boris' first name is actually Alexander and all his family refer to him by his first name, or Al.

☐ TRUE ☐ FALSE

4. As a boy Boris suffered from deafness. The affliction was caused by a build up of hair in his ear canal.

☐ TRUE ☐ FALSE

5. Boris is a huge admirer of Winston Churchill and has named his two sons after the man: Winston Chartwell Johnson and Churchill Blenheim Johnson.

☐ TRUE ☐ FALSE

6. Boris wasn't always the dyed-in-the-wool Tory he is today. During his time at Oxford he briefly aligned himself with the left-leaning Social Democratic Party.

☐ TRUE ☐ FALSE

REVOLUCIÓN

Answers: 1=true, 2=true, 3=true, 4=the deafness part is true, but the cause is false, 5=Boris loves Churchill but not enough to name his boys after him, 6=true

1. While at Oxford, Boris became heavily involved in the city's burgeoning rave scene. He started a fledgling record label, E-Tone funded by his school friend Charles Spencer, the brother of Princess Diana and heir to the Marks & Spencer retail empire.

☐ TRUE ☐ FALSE

2. During his time as a member of the Bullingdon Club, Boris Johnson witnessed future Prime Minister David Cameron simulate oral sex with a pig's head.

☐ TRUE ☐ FALSE

3. Boris was Margaret Thatcher's favorite journalist.

☐ TRUE ☐ FALSE

4. Following his firing from his job at *The Times* and before his hiring by *The Daily Telegraph*, Boris became addicted to the daytime soap *Neighbours*. To this day he ensures an aide records each episode so he can catch up later that evening. His favorite character is Dr Karl.

☐ TRUE ☐ FALSE

5. Boris is officially banned from French Polynesia following a piece he wrote in *The Telegraph* where he questioned the quality of their coconuts.

☐ TRUE ☐ FALSE

6. According to the *Oxford English Dictionary*, Boris is responsible for the growth in recognition of johnson as a slang term for a penis.

☐ TRUE ☐ FALSE

7. Boris is a keen tennis player and has publically challenged his namesake, Boris Becker to a game.

☐ TRUE ☐ FALSE

15

Answers: 1=false, 2=false—Boris wasn't there, and neither was Dave (allegedly), 3=true, 4=false, 5=false, 6=false, 7=true

1. A keen advocate of cycling, Boris names all his bikes after former girlfriends. His favorite is a fold-up bike called Allegra.

☐ TRUE ☐ FALSE

2. He loves violent films and his favorite movie of all time is Ben Stiller's *Dodgeball*.

☐ TRUE ☐ FALSE

3. Boris is a passionate classics scholar and was used as a consultant on the 2004 Brad Pitt movie *Troy*.

☐ TRUE ☐ FALSE

4. Boris was until recently an American citizen and has lots of family in the US. One distant relation is the actor and former wrestler Dwayne Johnson, aka The Rock.

☐ TRUE ☐ FALSE

Answers: 1=false, 2=true, 3=Boris is a passionate lassics scholar but had no involvement in Troy, 4=He was formerly a US citizen but he is not related to The Rock

1. In 1998, following his first appearance on *Have I Got News for You*, Boris was approached as a possible star of a Just for Men hair dye advertising campaign.

☐ TRUE ☐ FALSE

2. Boris is a huge fan of the Rolling Stones, stating that Keith Richards is "the man" and attempting as a teenager to dress like his guitar hero.

☐ TRUE ☐ FALSE

3. Speaking of guitar heroes, Boris's third cousin is Brian Johnson from the rock band AC/DC.

☐ TRUE ☐ FALSE

4. Boris created a Johnson family crest with the motto *"canis meus id comedit,"* which translates as "my dog ate it."

☐ TRUE ☐ FALSE

5. Before each public engagement, Boris insists on the presence of a stylist who can make him look suitably disheveled.

☐ TRUE ☐ FALSE

6. According to Petronella Wyatt, with whom Boris had an affair, he's a bit of a loner but is desperate to be liked, he doesn't enjoy parties, and believes that monogamy is a very unreasonable proposition.

☐ TRUE ☐ FALSE

Answers: 1=false, 2=true, 3=false, 4=false, 5=false, 6=true

Boris On...

Here is a selection of some of Boris's best quotes.

On Hillary Clinton:

"She's got dyed blonde hair and pouty lips, and a steely blue stare, like a sadistic nurse in a mental hospital."

On the Turkish President Tayyip Erdogan:

"...a terrific wankerer..."

On Winston Churchill:

"He was dressed in his strange Victorian/Edwardian garb... like some burly and hungover butler from the set of Downton Abbey."

On David Cameron:

"I am supporting David Cameron purely out of cynical self-interest."

On Donald Trump:

"'The only reason I wouldn't visit some parts of New York is the real risk of meeting Donald Trump."

On Nicola Sturgeon:

"Voracious weevil"

On Alan Johnson MP standing down as Shadow Chancellor:

"I will greatly miss Alan Johnson, not just because he is a nice guy but also for the satisfaction I used to get when I saw a headline saying, 'Johnson in new gaffe' and realized it wasn't me."

On the UK Independence Party:

"I can hardly condemn UKIP as a bunch of boss-eyed, foam-flecked Euro hysterics, when I have been sometimes not far short of boss-eyed, foam-flecked hysteria myself."

On the Commonwealth:

"It is said that the Queen has come to love the Commonwealth, partly because it supplies her with regular cheering crowds of flag-waving piccaninnies"

On China:

"Chinese cultural influence is virtually nil, and unlikely to increase..."

On Portsmouth:

"Here we are in one of the most depressed towns in southern England, a place that is arguably too full of drugs, obesity, underachievement and Labour MPs."

On Las Vegas:

"I think it'd be disgraceful if a chap wasn't allowed to have a bit of fun in Las Vegas. The real scandal would be if you went all the way to Las Vegas and you didn't misbehave in some trivial way."

On Europe:

"I certainly want a European community where one can go off and scoff croissants, drink delicious coffee, learn foreign languages and generally make love to foreign women."

On drugs:

"I think I was once given cocaine but I sneezed so it didn't go up my nose. In fact, it may have been icing sugar."

On cake:

"My policy on cake is pro having it and pro eating it."

On dieting:

"I'm kicking off my diet with cheeseburger-whatever Jamie Oliver says McDonalds are incredibly nutritious and, as far as I can tell, crammed full of vital nutrients and rigid with goodness."

On fast cars:

"How does it hurt me, with my 20-year-old Toyota, if somebody else has a swish Mercedes? We both get stuck in the same traffic."

On the media:

"It is possible to have a pretty good life and career being a leech and a parasite in the media world, gadding about from TV studio to TV studio, writing inconsequential pieces and having a good time."

On his hair:

"You can say what you like about my hairstyle, but it's never caused epilepsy and cost significantly less than £400,000 to design."

On being PM:

"My realistic chances of becoming Prime Minister are only slightly better than my chances of being decapitated by a frisbee, blinded by a champagne cork, locked in a disused fridge, or reincarnated as an olive"

Boris vs

A few sharp observations on dear old Boris.

"Boris Johnson: the thinking man's idiot."

Radio presenter and musician Humphrey Lyttelton

"I wish it was a joke, but I fear it isn't."

Former Swedish Prime Minister Carl Bildt on learning about Boris's appointment as foreign secretary

"He's not really in politics, Boris Johnson, to make your life better. He's certainly not in politics to make my life better. Boris Johnson is in politics to make Boris Johnson's life better. First, last and always..."

LBC radio host James O'Brien

"It's not his clothes and coiffure, but his personality that makes him look as if he has been rolled on by a horse and then seduced by it."
Author and broadcaster Clive James

"Boris Johnson is the human equivalent of the bendy bus: looks like fun but essentially is dangerous and annoying."
Writer and comedian Sharon Horgan

"Boris act[s] like Trump with a thesaurus."
Former leader of the Liberal Democrat party Nick Clegg

"People always ask me the same question, they say, 'Is Boris a very, very clever man pretending to be an idiot?' And I always say, 'No.'"

Journalist and satirist Ian Hislop

"If Boris Johnson gets elected it would be a case of the lunatic having no clue how to run the asylum."

Actor Alan Rickman

"He may seem like a loveable buffoon but you know he wouldn't hesitate to line you all up against a wall and have you shot."

Comedian Jeremy Hardy

"Boris as mayor? Lovely to see other comedians getting work, but four years is a bit long for a comedy routine." Comedian David Mitchell

"A fairly lazy tosser who just wants to be there." Former London Mayor Ken Livingstone

"It's quite well studied, the whole hair business. I've seen him come out of make-up with his hair perfectly combed and 15 seconds later it's like this [mimes unruly hair]. And he's done it himself." Comedian Paul Merton

"Boris Johnson look[s] like a Harry Potter spell that's brought all the hair in Dumbledore's plughole to life" Comedian Frankie Boyle

"He's the sort of person who 200 years ago would have died aged 30 leading a cavalry charge into a volcano." And one more from Frankie Boyle

Dress up Boris!

Boris has got a busy day ahead of him. Get the Prime Minister ready for an important day at the Houses of Parliament.

Nest hair?

Patriotic T-shirt?

Troll hair?

Smart suit?

Cycle lycra

That's Not My Hair!

Boris is having a particularly bad hair day. Can you identify the six items masquerading as his haircut?

34

5

4

6

Answers: 1=angora rabbit, 2=household mop,
3=Andy Warhol's wig, 4=a bird's nest,
5=a needle in a haystack, 6=nuclear mushroom cloud

35

Zippedy Doo Dah

Not satisfied with his experience during the London Olympics, Boris has got himself stuck on a zip wire again.

Can you untangle it to get him down?

The Great Scandal Escape

1 2 3 4

YOU ARE PURSUED BY PAPS OVER RUMOURS OF A LOVE CHILD.

GO BACK 2 SPACES

20 18 17 16

OH NO, A PUNCTURE!

LOSE A TURN

21

22 23

A LIBEL CASE GOES IN YOUR FAVOUR.

GO FORWARD 3 SPACES

25 26

Hold the front page! Boris is in a spot of bother again with the press and needs to get back to the Houses of Parliament ASAP to limit the damage. Can he make it in time? Roll the dice and find out.

6 7 8 9

YOU ESCAPE THE PRESS USING A BORIS BIKE.

GO FORWARD 2 SPACES

GO BACK 2 SPACES

UNDERGROUND ON STRIKE!

THE PROTESTING TUBE DRIVERS ARE ON STRIKE.

14 13 12

11

27 28 29

HOME

Lost for Words

Find as many of these Boris-related words and phrases as you can:

Piffle	Hair
Sorry	Oxford
Wiff Waff	Bullingdon
Bike	Bendy Bus
Affair	Tory
Zip	Jelly
Brexit	Euro
London	Mayor
Gaffe	Livingstone
Eton	Gove
Latin	Et Tu Brute
Telegraph	Editor
Elect	PM
Tennis	

B	R	E	X	I	T	R	O	T	I	D	E
E	K	I	B	Y	E	F	F	A	G	T	E
B	U	L	L	I	N	G	D	O	N	E	N
A	E	O	M	Z	N	W	C	E	Q	L	O
D	U	N	H	P	I	F	F	L	E	E	T
J	R	D	D	G	S	P	X	E	J	G	S
N	O	O	R	Y	R	O	T	C	E	R	G
I	O	N	F	O	B	I	R	T	L	A	N
T	H	T	Y	X	Y	U	A	R	L	P	I
A	P	A	E	V	O	G	S	F	Y	H	V
L	M	W	I	F	F	W	A	F	F	A	I
Y	E	T	U	R	B	U	T	T	E	A	L

Boris's
Brexit Maze

The votes have been counted and the referendum has been won—Britain has voted to leave the European Union. But how will it get out of there?

Guide Boris toward his "friends" Nigel and Jacob and safely out of the EU, avoiding any confrontations with those pesky Europhiles.

Who is Boris Insulting?

Match the person to the insult Boris hurled at them.

1. Despite looking a bit like Dobby the House Elf, he is a ruthless and manipulative tyrant.

2. He is a mixture of Harry Houdini and a greased piglet. He is barely human in his elusiveness.

3. ... some photographers were trying to take a picture of me and a girl walked down the pavement towards me and she stopped and she said, 'Gee is that _____?' It was one of the worst moments."

4. "A cross-eyed ... warmonger, unelected, inarticulate, who epitomizes the arrogance of ... foreign policy."

44

Answers: 1=D, 2=B, 3=A, 4=C

A. Donald Trump

B. Tony Blair

C. George W. Bush

D. Vladimir Putin

Dear Boris...

Never too shy to dole out advice, here are excerpts from Boris's agony aunt columns, where he offers counsel to his peers and colleagues in the political establishment.

Dear Boris, I recently lost my job (thanks for that by the way) and my lovely husband is already tired of having me around the house all day. Any suggestions? *Mrs "T", Berkshire*

Dear T, what can I say, it was a pleasure. I am always free for a spot of retail therapy. Just say the word and I can jump on a Boris bike and meet you in Westfield shopping mall in half an hour. I hear there are plenty of shoe shops there we can visit. *Boris*

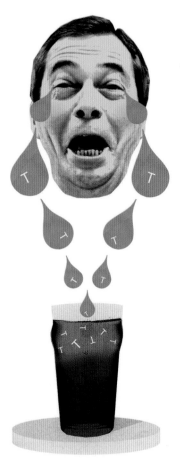

"Dear Boris, I recently achieved my life's ambition (thanks for that by the way), but now I have nothing to do all day but visit the pub, and nobody there will talk to me since they realized that their villas on the Costa del Crime are in jeopardy. How can I get them to like me again?"

Big Nige from Thanet

"Dear Nige, Sorry mate, they never liked you in the first place." *Boris*

"Dear Boris, having become something of a Brexit figurehead (thanks for that by the way), my diary is full to bursting with speaking engagements at Conservative clubs across the land. The trouble is, Nanny doesn't like me staying out later than 8pm. How can I get her to let me go?" *Jacob, aged 49 and three quarters*

"Dear Jakey, this is a question of personal sovereignty. Brexit will not be stopped by any nanny, so grow up! Audentes Fortuna iuvat and all that." *Boris*

"Dear Boris, I'm suffering a real crisis of confidence (thanks for that by the way). One minute I'm down with the kids and they are singing my name at Glastonbury, the next nobody wants to be my friend. What am I doing wrong?" *Jez, Islington*

"Dear Jez, the youth really are a fickle bunch. How about trying to appease them by making a load of populist promises you know you definitely won't keep. Works for me!" *Boris*

"Hey Boris, Greetings from the greatest country on earth! I'm pretty new to this politics game but by following your example I have managed to convince a LOT of people that I'm not simply a rich loudmouth buffoon (thanks for that by the way) and am indeed capable of running a country. The problem is I've made a promise to build a wall that's basically impossible to fulfil, what can I do to get out of it?" *The Donald, NYC baby!*

"Dear Mr The Donald, it's amazing what pointless follies you can turn into reality with a bit of PMA. I've wasted hundreds of millions on plenty of white elephants—a $60 million cable car used regularly by only four people for example. Follow your dreams—it's easy if you know the right people. Good luck!" *Boris*

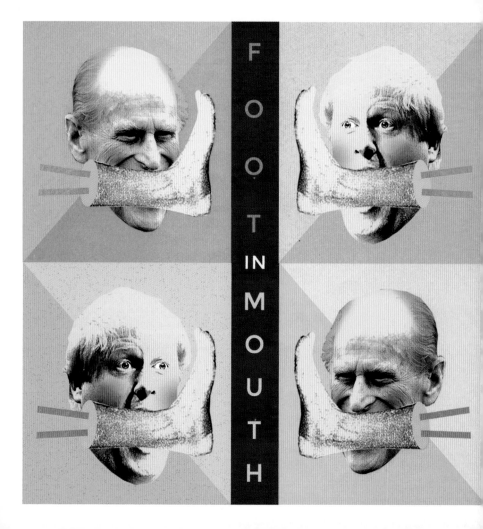

"Dear Boris, I've done it again and put my foot in it with a load of bloody spear chuckers… Er, sorry, ethnics from the colonies. No, that's not it either. Well, I've ballsed it up by insulting whatever the PC brigade call them these days. Often you've stepped in with your own gaffes that really take the heat off (thanks for that by the way), but how do you always get away with it?"

Phil, Balmoral

"Dear Phil, to be honest I have no idea. If I knew the answer to that question I'd be a rich man. Oh hang on, I already am. Jolly good!" *Boris*

Learn Latin *with Boris*

A few choice phrases mastered in the libraries of Oxford.

Pro patria mori.... stuff my country, I'm going for glory

Princeps esse velim.... oh lord, have I actually got to stand for leader now?

Amo, amas, amat.... I love myself, I love you, I love her.... but mostly myself

Et tu Michael.... I've walked into a massive elephant trap here.

PLAYING

Boris: A Sporting Life

Over the course of his time in the public eye, Boris has never shied away from demonstrating his sporting prowess. Here are a few of his sporting highlights, imagined in the voice of Boris's diary.

Rugby

Bit of an oopsie today. While on a trip to Tokyo I was invited to take part in a game of touch rugby with some Japanese children. Sadly the old competitive streak couldn't be restrained, as I imagined myself back on the playing fields of Eton, pulling on the school colors and representing the first 15, gallantly channeling Achilles leading the Myrmidons as I commanded the field. Sadly, the boys I was up against hadn't prepared themselves for the trademark BoJo Bulldozer and a poor bugger got in my way—and I sent the scamp flying. Luckily (for me) the boy wasn't injured (too badly) and the press saw the funny side. Result!

Football

Did my bit for charity today by dusting off the old boots to take part in a charity kick about against the Jerries. I'm not known for my footballing skills, having not played since leaving the old alma mater, but still, one has to grab any chance to line up against the Krauts. With 10 minutes left on the clock I was off the subs bench and on the pitch, taking my earliest opportunity to bosh one of the Bosch with a well-timed head-first tackle on Maurizio Gaudino. Well, I've never made it a secret that I was more of a rugby fan, what did they expect?

Cycling

There I am riding along the newly opened segregated section of London's cycle superhighway, a majestic throughfare that straddles the Thames like the Colossus of Rhodes, when a cyclist comes towards me with middle digit extended. Having tirelessly campaigned for the opening of this route, having caused aggro with many old Buller chums who resented their chauffeurs being held up by road works, having tried to ameliorate the lives of those who take to two wheels, the picture that gets in the papers is me being abused by the cyclists I'm trying to help. Not since Jason abandoned Medea has there been a betrayal so great. : (

Table tennis

The cat is truly among the pigeons today. I'm in China, representing the city of London at the closing ceremony of the Beijing Olympics, and appear to have caused the single biggest upset to Sino-British relations since the Daoguang Emperor refused to legalise opium. Sadly, the Chinese didn't take well to being reminded of the fact that table tennis, or wiff-waff as it was originally known, was invented on the dining tables of Victorian England and it was my job to bring the sport back to London. According to the local (red) rags, I'm culturally insensitive, rude, arrogant and disrespectful. I didn't realize they knew me so well over there! Still, at least they didn't bring up my column where I described their cultural influence as virtually nil.

What Would Boris Do?

Channel your inner Boris and take this simple quiz to see if you too could be a BoJo.

1. You are elected Prime Minister, with responsibility for a budget of billions of pounds. Do you:

A. Buy a calculator and try to work out how to spend the money to the benefit of the majority of UK citizens.

B. Snigger every time someone says the word 'million'?

C. Sign a book deal with a major publishing house for a six-figure advance, on the understanding that you will include juicy titbits about Theresa May.

2. You take a principled political stand that alienates your entire family. Do you:

A. Make a reasonable and considered argument for your apparent about-face from the values you were raised with.

B. Ring up your sister and shout 'Nah nah nah nah nah' down the phone at her.

C. Start planning Bullingdon-style parties to be held at 10 Downing Street once you are Prime Minister.

3. You may or may not have had an extra-marital affair which neither your wife nor the British press have found out about yet. Do you:

A. Decide to end it before there is any damage to your marriage or career.

B. Carry on—you can't believe your luck!

C. Wait until you are found out and then deny everything.

4. On a trip abroad, you inadvertently offend an entire nation. Do you:

A. Apologize profusely on their national TV channel.

B. Decide to leave, but accidentally knock over a small child with your luggage trolley at the airport.

C. Make an apology but then ruin it by coming out with an even worse insult while apologizing.

Check your results overleaf...

What Would Boris Do? : Results

Mostly As: you are far too serious, you need to lighten up a bit (and possibly dye your hair blond).

Mostly Bs: this is much more promising, you are more like a young Boris (but you do need to dye your hair very blond).

Mostly Cs: congratulations, you could stand in for Boris any day (as long as you dye your hair blond).

Acknowledgments

The publisher would like to thank Blair Frame for his excellent and very speedy illustrations, and Geoff Borin for his excellent and very speedy design. Thanks also to Boris Johnson for inspiring us all.